William Girdlestone Shellabear

The Singapore Triglot Vocabulary

William Girdlestone Shellabear

The Singapore Triglot Vocabulary

ISBN/EAN: 9783337386115

Printed in Europe, USA, Canada, Australia, Japan

Cover: Foto ©Paul-Georg Meister /pixelio.de

More available books at **www.hansebooks.com**

THE
SINGAPORE TRIGLOT VOCABULARY.

COMPILED BY

WILLIAM G. SHELLABEAR,

late Royal Engineers.

THE CHINESE RENDERINGS BY

Rev. B. F. WEST, M.D.

SINGAPORE:

Printed at the "American Mission Press."

1891.

ALL RIGHTS RESERVED.

PREFACE.

At the outset this vocabulary was designed chiefly for the use of boys who are learning English in the lower Standards in the Schools of the Straits Settlements, but as soon as the work of compilation was commenced it appeared advisable to so arrange the words that the book might be more widely useful.

The great majority of boys in these Settlements learn English through the medium of Malay, not the Malay of the Malays, but what may almost be termed a dialect, commonly known by the name of Bazaar, Colloquial or Low Malay. Many of the words used in Colloquial Malay are not used at all by the Malays themselves, or are used in a different sense; it has however been necessary to admit such words and expressions into this vocabulary in order to make it useful in schools and among the Malay-speaking Chinese, but to distinguish them from pure Malay words the abbreviation *(col)* has been inserted after them.

In order to avoid needlessly confusing the minds of those who are beginning the study of the English language, it has been sought as far as possible to avoid uncommon and difficult words; and great pains have been taken where an English word has several different meanings, not only to give the correct renderings in Malay, but also to give an equivalent English word in order to explain the sense in which it is used.

To the student of the Malay language we do not pretend to offer a complete list of Malay words, but by far the greater number of Europeans who come to the East require only a small vocabulary of words in order to transact their business and communicate with their servants; for such we believe that this collection of words will be amply sufficient, and even those who propose to make a deeper study of the language will find this book a stepping stone to the more complete and more expensive works on the Malay language.

Affixes and prefixes really constitute the Grammar of the Malay language, but they are almost entirely omitted in Colloquial Malay; for this reason they have been used as little as possible in this work, but it is intended to add a short article on the use of affixes and prefixes in the form of an appendix or as a separate book. The affix *kan*, by means of which transitive verbs are formed from intransitive verbs or other parts of speech, has however been frequently used in order to avoid the excessive use of *kasi*, which is very incorrect; thus *masokkan* is given for *to put in*, instead of *kasi masok* which is so frequently used. Wherever an English verb has both a transitive and intransitive meaning, the Malay of the intransitive meaning is given first, thus: *to increase—tambah; tambahkan.*

The addition of the Chinese renderings, which is one great feature of this work, will it is hoped make the book useful not only to the Malay speaking Chinese who are studying the Chinese language, but also to the Chinese merchants and others who come here from their own country with a desire to learn something both of English and Malay, without which they find it impossible to transact their business. I am very much indebted to Dr. West for the time and trouble which he has devoted to the difficult work of translating and proofreading this portion of the work, which it would have been quite impossible to have undertaken without his assistance.

W. G. S.

SINGAPORE,
September, 1891.

MALAY TRANSLITERATION

AND

PRONUNCIATION.

───◆───

The system of transliteration used in this book is believed to be different from any other system hitherto used for Malay in Roman letters, but it is so similar in general principles to the system now universally adopted for Romanizing the Chinese languages, and has already been so thoroughly tested in various ways that we are confident of its utility.

In this system it is sought to spell the words as nearly as may be phonetically, but entirely without the use of accents, and adhering as nearly as possible to the spelling of the words in the Arabic Character.

It will at once be noticed that the main difference between this and previous systems is the omission of vowels in such words as: *bgini, lkas, mngaku,* where no vowel occurs in the Arabic Character. *Bgini* has previously been variously spelt as follows: *bagini, băgini, begini, bĕgini, bugini, bŭgini,* from which it would tax the powers of the average learner to select the true pronunciation. It is claimed and has frequently been proved that such words as *bgini* and *lkas*, when shown to a European who is ignorant of Malay, are at once correctly pronounced. The forms *mng* and *png* appear more difficult at first sight, but such combinations of letters are frequent in Romanized Chinese, and present no difficulty whatever when the system is thoroughly understood. The vowel *e* has in almost every case been retained before *r*, because there is no danger in such cases of the syllable being wrongly pronounced, and reading is facilitated by the addition of the vowel. The letter *y* has been used to distinguish the Malay letter *nya* from the combination of the two letters *n* and *i*, thus: *punya, dunia.* The letter *y* has also been used where there is distinctly a *ya yi* or *yu* sound, and similarly *w* has been used where there is a *wa we* or *wi* sound, for example: *yang, Yusof, aniaya; wakil, werna, bawa.*

Wherever *ain*, the Arabic nasal *a*, occurs in the Arabic Character, it is indicated by the use of the apostrophe, thus: *a'dat, do'a;* and the same mark is also used to indicate the letter *hamza*, which has the force of a breathing, thus: *Kora'an, mla'ikat, poko'.*

In words which are compounds of *s-*, *one*, or *k-*, *to*, or *di-*, *at*, or *di-*, *the form of past participle*, and some other word, the hyphen has been retained, because those prefixes are really separate words, as: *s-kjap, k-sana, di-sini, di-pukol;* and similarly the affixes *-lah, -kah, -tah, -nah, -nya, -ku, -mu,* are hyphened as being really separate words. But where the prefix or affix forms really part of the word, the hyphen is not used, thus: *bergrak, grakkan, makanan.*

The consonants in Malay are pronounced as in English, except that the *r* should be sounded very much more than an Englishman usually does. The consonants *ng* represent one letter in Malay, and should be pronounced as in *singer*, never as in *single;* the latter sound is given in Malay by the addition of a *g*, thus *singa*, a *lion; singgah, to call in at a place.* So also *ungu* is not *un-gu*, but *ung-u.* Final *k* in Malay is not pronounced, but whenever it occurs the final syllable must be pronounced very short indeed. Final *h* and *hamza* have also the effect of shortening the last syllable, but they have not more than half the effect of final *k*.

The vowels are pronounced as in Italian, thus: *a* as in *father*, but not always with the same degree of hardness, for instance in the word *padang*, the first *a* is pronounced a good deal harder than the second. In *kahandak* and similar words the *a* has been retained between the *k* and *h* to distinguish from the Arabic guttural *kh;* the *a* must be pronounced very short.

When *e* comes before *r* pronounce as in *perhaps;*

example, *berkat*. The words *merah, perak*, etc., are however exceptions to this rule, and should rather perhaps be spelt as they are pronounced, viz :—*meyrah, peyrak;* the *ey* as in *they.* Elsewhere *e* has always the sound of *ey* in *they;* examples, *Esok, tengo', bengko', adek, boleh.* In the word *negri* the *e* has only been left in to prevent the *n* and *g* coming together and forming *ng-ri*, in this word the *e* should be pronounced as short as possible.

Pronounce *i* as in *ravine*, or as *ee* in *feet;* example *kaki, kipas.* At the end of a word, when followed by a consonant, *i* is pronounced as in *bit;* example, *gigit, angin.*

Pronounce *o* as in *hole*, example, *boleh, suroh.*

Pronounce *u* as in *June*, example, *upah, budak.*

The sound of *o* or *u* in the last syllable of many words is however half way between the above *o* and *u* sounds, so that some persons write an *o* and others a *u*, for instance *pikol* or *pikul, ikut* or *ikot, turot* or *turut, rambot* or *rambut.* It matters little which way these words are written, the true pronunciation of them can only be got from a native.

When two vowels come together both must be sounded, but the first must be run more or less into the second, thus *au* gets nearly the sound of *ow* in *cow*, as *pisau, mau;* and *ai* has the sound of the English *i* in *ice*, thus: *sungai, pakai, kdai.*

VOCABULARY.

English.	Malay.	Chinese.
A	satu *or* s-	一
Able, to be	boleh	能干
About (concerning)	deri-hal; fasal	差將項無務事涉不
About (nearly)	kira-kira	
About to, to be	nanti; mau *(col)*	多欲
Above	atas	面在
Absent	tidak ada	的
Abuse, to	maki	
Accept, to	trima	受
Accounts	kira-kira	賬項
Accurate (correct)	btul	着
Accustomed	biasa	慣勢
Ache	sakit	痛

Acid	asam	酸
Acknowledge, to	mngaku	認彼做
Across	sbrang	平行、
Act, to	buat	做
Add, to (increase)	tambah	添
Add up, to	jmlahkan	結
Advice	nasihat	教
Afraid	takot	懼
After (of place)	di-blakang	後
After (of time)	lpas	了
Afternoon	ptang	下晡
Afterwards	kmdian	後來
Again	lagi s-kali ; pula	再
Age	umor	歲
Ago	sudah	前
Agree, to	s-tuju	和
Aim, to	tuju	相
Air	udara	精氣
Alike	s-rupa	相像
Alive	hidop	活
All	smoa	總

SINGAPORE TRIGLOT VOCABULARY.   13

All right!	baik-lah	好
Allow, to	biar	准
Almost	hampir	差不多
Alone	s'orang sahaja	孤單的
Also	juga	亦在再
Alter, to	ubah; tukar	改
Altogether	s-kali-kali	盡
Always	slalu	常
Among	antara	中央
An	satu *or* s-	一
Anchor	sauh	錠
Anchor, to	berlaboh	拋錠
And	dan; pun	與
Angel	mla'ikat	天使
Angry	marah	怒氣
Animal	binatang	野獸牲畜
Another	lain satu; lagi satu	別個 一個
Answer	jawab	答復
Ant	smut	螞蟻
Ant (large red)	keringga	紅蟻
Any one	barang-siapa	隨便人

Anything	apa-apa	物、荀出
Appear, to	nampak	且現出
Argue, to	berbantah	論辯
Arise, to	bangun; bangkit	來起
Arithmetic	kira-kira	學數
Arm	tangan	手
Army	tntara	骨手排、四排
Around	kliling	陣圍列、
Arrange, to	atur	
Arrive, to	sampai	到至
As	sperti; macham	相似
Ashamed	malu	羞恥
Ask, to (enquire)	tanya	問
Ask for, to	minta; pinta	討
Asleep	tidor	睡值
Assist, to	tolong	助幫
At	pada; di	在
At first	mula-mula	先當
At once	skarang ini; lkas	緊、今試
Attempt, to	choba	看
Auction	lelong	嘟犁

Aunt	mak saudara	姑、姨
Await, to	nantikan	等候
Axe	kapak	斧頭
Baby	anak-kchil	嬰仔
Back	blakang	尻脊
Back, at the	di-blakang	後面
Back, to the	k-blakang	去後面
Back again	kmbali	到後來
Backwards	k-blakang	返後
Bad (of things)	kurang baik	不好
Bad (of men)	jahat	惡
Bad (rotten)	busok	朽爛
Bag	saku	袋
Baker	tukang-roti	賣麵包者
Ball	bola	毬
Bamboo	buloh	竹
Banana	pisang	芭蕉
Barber	tukang-chukor	剃頭司阜
Barrel	tong	桶
Basin	mangko' bsar	碗盆、
Basket	bakul	筐籃、

Bathe, to	mandi	洗浴
Bath-room	tmpat-mandi	浴房
Bazaar	pasar	街市
Be, to	ada; jadi	是、做
Beam	balak	楹
Beans	kachang	荳
Bear, to (endure)	tahan	吞忍
Beard	janggot	嘴鬚
Beat, to	pukol	打
Beautiful	chantek; bagus	好看
Because	kerna; sbab	因爲
Become, to	mnjadi	做成
Bed	tmpat-tidor	眠床
Beef	daging lmbu	牛肉
Before (of time)	dhulu	先前
Before (of place)	di-hadapan	尙面
Before (ere)	s-blum	起未
Begin, to	mula'i	頭正
Beginning	mula; permula'an	頭面
Behaviour	klakuan	品行
Behind	di-blakang	後面

Behove, to	patut	應該
Believe, to (trust)	perchaya	信
Believe, to (think)	fikir	想, 打筭
Bell	loching	鐘
Belly	prot	腹肚
Belt	tali pinggang	帶
Below	di-bawah	下邊
Bench	bangku	椅條
Bent	bengko'	拗蹺
Beside	di-s-blah	邊仔面
Best	yang terlbeh baik	第一好
Better	lbeh baik	更好
Between	antara	中央
Beyond	di-s-blah	邊仔
Beyond (water)	sbrang	那旁
Bible	Kitab Allah	聖冊
Big	bsar	大
Bill	surat hutang	單
Bird	burong	鳥
Bit, a (piece)	s-kping	一塊
Bit (for horses)	lagam	馬咬轡

Bite	gigit	咬
Black	hitam	烏
Blacksmith	tukang-bsi	鐵司阜
Blessing	berkat	祝福
Blind	buta	青瞑
Blood	darah	血
Blow, to	tiop	噴、吹
Blue	biru	藍
Blunt	tumpol	鈍
Board	papan	朽
Boat	prahu; sampan	船仔
Body	badan	身軀
Boil, to	rbus; masak (col)	煮
Bolt	kanching	鑽
Bone	tulang	骨
Book	kitab; buku (col)	册
Boot	spatu	靴
Born	beranak (col)	出世
Borrow, to	pinjam	借
Both	dua-dua	二個
Bough	dahan	幹

SINGAPORE TRIGLOT VOCABULARY.   19

Box	pti	箱、盒子
Boy	budak	男童、仔
Brass	tmbaga	銅
Brave	brani	好胆
Bread	roti	麵包
Break, to	pchah; patah; putus	破、折、斷
Breakfast	makan-pagi	食早起前
Breast	dada	胸
Breath	nafas	氣
Brick	batu-bata	雙
Bribe, a	suap	買嘱
Bride	pngantin prempuan	新娘
Bridge	jmbatan	橋
Bring, to	bawa	挪帶
Broad	lebar	濶
Broom	pnyapu	苕掃
Brother	saudara	兄弟
Brother, elder	abang	兄
Brother, younger	adek	弟
Brother-in-law	ipar	大小舅
Brush	brus	刷

Bucket	timba; tong	桶水造
Buffalo	kerbau	仔牛椿
Build, to	buat; bangunkan	牛仔束
Bullock	lmbu	起杭燒
Bullock-cart	kreta lmbu	仔車埋
Bump, a	bngkak	着事
Bundle	bungkus	捆若
Burn, to	bakar	牛
Bury, to	tanam; kuborkan	葬鈕
Business	kerja	路頭是買
But	ttapi	乳對
Butter	mntega	油仔少
Button	kanching	餅
Buy, to	bli	叫
By	oleh	攔
By and by	lagi s-kjap	停探
Cake	pnganan; kweh (col)	喊
Call, to (call for)	panggil	
Call in, to (at a place)	singgah	
Call on, to (visit)	mlawat	
Call out, to	triak	叫

Can (able)	boleh	能
Candle	dian; lilin *(col)*	灼蠟、灼
Cane	rotan	籐
Cannot	ta'boleh	不得
Cap	kopiah	帽
Care, to	fduli	要緊
Care, to take	jaga	仔細
Care of, to take	pliharakan	照顧
Careless, to be	lalai	苶董司
Carpenter	tukang-kayu	木
Carriage	kreta	車
Cart	kreta	車
Carry	angkat *(col)*	取
,, (on the hands)	tatang	挑
,, (on the head)	junjong	戴
,, (on the hips)	dukong	夯
,, (on the shoulder)	pikul	扛
Cash	wang	銀
Cashier	tukang-wang	銀櫃
Cat	kuching	猫
Catch, to	tangkap	擒、掠

Cause, a	sbab	緣、俾、中的、某有 故
Cause, to	jadikan; buat	
Centre	tngah	、間、確、人、粟、鍊、椅、白、改 做
Certain (positive)	tntu	
Certain man, a	s'orang anu	換、代、搬、章、心 着、定、
Chaff	skam	
Chain	rantai	
Chair	kursi; krusi	
Chalk	kapur blanda	土、換、字、火
Change, to, (alter)	ubah	
,, to (exchange)	tukar	
,, to (substitute)	gantikan	
Change house, to	pindah	
Chapter	fasal	
Character (behaviour)	klakuan; prangai	地、炭、道、捷、俗、騙
Character (letter)	surat	
Charcoal	arang	
Chase, to	kjar	
Chatter, to	bising	講、捷
Cheap	murah	
Cheat, to	tipu	

Cheese	keju	牛乳餅
Chicken	ayam	雞仔
Child	anak	子童
Chisel	pahat	鑿
Choose	pileh	揀選
Christ	Almasih	基督耶穌
Christian	msihi	信主教
,, (R. Catholic)	nserani	天主堂
Church	greja	禮拜堂
City	negri	城
Clay	tanah liat	土
Clean	berseh	清
Clean, to	chuchi	清氣
Clear	trang	明
Clerk	krani	記
Clever	pandai	夥賢
Climb	panjat	拍
Clock	jam	時鐘
Close	dkat; rapat	近
Close, to	tutop	開合
Cloth	kain	布

Clothes	pakian	衣裳
Cloud	awan	雲
Coal	arang batu	土炭
Coarse	kasar	粗
Coat	baju	衫
Cock	ayam jantan	雞牡
Cocoa-nut	klapa	椰
Cocoa-nut milk	ayer klapa	椰乳
Coffee	kopi *(col)*	高卑
Coffin	long; pti orang mati *(col)*	棺柴
Cold	sjuk; dingin	寒冷
Colour	werna	色
Collect, to	kumpol; kampongkan	聚堆做却集
Comb	sikat	梳
Come!	mari	來
Come, to	datang	來
Come in, to	masok	入來
Command	hukum	戒命
Commence, to	mula'i	起
Compare, to	bandingkan	比
Concerning	deri-hal; fasal	論

Condemn, to (sentence)	hukumkan	
,, to (to blame)	salahkan	
Conduct	klakuan	
Confess, to	mngaku	
Conquer, to	mnang; alahkan	
Conscience	s-tau-hati	
Contain, to	muat; isi	
Contents	isi	
Convenient	snang	
Cook	kuki	
Cook, to	masak	
Copy, to (transcribe)	salin	
Copy, to (imitate)	turut	
Copper	tmbaga	
Cork	pnyumbat	
Corn	gandom	
Corner (of a room)	pnjuru	
Corner (of a street)	sempang	
Correct, to	btulkan	
Correct	btul	
Cost	herga	

擬責德認較良財所順煮煮抄學紅草五角改著價
罪備行　贏　心　　便食　　銅谷　角　錢
嫌、　　　　　　　物之粧　　
　　　　　　　　　者　食

Cotton	kapas	棉紗
Cotton, sewing	bnang	花線
Count, to	hitong; bilang	算數
Country	negri; bnua	國
Courage	brani	胆
Cover, to	tutop; tudong	遮盖
Cow	lmbu btina	牛
Coward	pnakot	無人之胆
Crab	ktam	蟳
Create, to	jadikan	造創
Crooked	bengko'	曲
Cross	marah	怒氣
Cross (ancient method of execution) salib		十字架
Crowd	kumpolan	羣
Crucify, to	salibkan	釘十字架
Cruel	bngis	殘忍
Cry, to (to weep)	mnangis; tangis	哮大聲
Cry, to (to call out)	bertriak	叫喉
Cup	mangko'	甌
Cure, to	sumboh	醫
Curse, to	kutok	詛咒

Curtain	tirai	帳
Curtain, mosquito	klambu	蚊帳
Custom	'adat	風俗
Cut, to	potong	割
Daily	s-hari-hari	日日
Damage, to	rosak	打濕
Damp	lmbab	投濕
Dance, to	mnari	跳
Danger	bahia	危險
Daring	brani	好膽
Dark	glap	暗
Date	hari-bulan	日期
Daughter	anak prempuan	某子
Day	hari	日
Day, mid-	tngah-hari	高午
Day after to-morrow	lusa	後日
Day-light	siang	日時
Dead	mati	死
Deaf	pkak; tuli	聾耳
Dear (in price)	mhal	貴
Death	kmatian	死

Debt	hutang	欠債
Deceive, to	tipu	瞞騙
Deep	dalam	深
Defeat, to	alahkan	剉嬴
Delay, to	lambat	停延遲
Deliver, to (set free)	lpaskan	救放
Deliver up, to (hand over)	srahkan	交
Demon	hantu; jin	鬼
Deny, to	mungkir	不認
Deserve, to	patut	應該
Desire, to	mau; berkahandak	愛要
Desk	meja-tulis	寫字棹
Destroy, to	binasakan	滅無
Devil, the	Shaitan; Iblis	魔鬼
Die, to	mati	過往
Difference	berlainan	分別
Different	lain	異樣
Difficult	susah	難
Dig, to	gali	掘
Diligent	rajin	勤
Direct	trus	直

Dirt	kotor	污穢
Dirt (loose)	sampah	驚人
Dirty	kotor	驚人
Disgrace	malu	俾人見誚
Dish	pinggan	盤
Dislike, to	ta'suka	恨
Dismiss, to	kluarkan	辭
Distance	jauh	遠
Disturbance	gadoh	擾亂
Ditch	parit	溝
Dive, to	slam	寐水
Divide, to (distribute)	bhagi	分
Divide, to (cut in two)	blah	切
Do, to	buat	做行
Doctor	dukun; doctor (col)	醫生員
Dog	anjing	狗
Dollar	ringgit	一員
Done (finished)	sudah	明白
Donkey	kaldai	驢可
Dont!	jangan	不
Door	pintu	門

Double	dua-kali	重班
Dove	merpati	鳩
Down	bawah	下
Down (at)	di-bawah	下底
Down (to)	k-bawah	下脚
Down, to go	turun	下樓
Dozen, a	dua-blas; dusin *(col)*	一羅
Drain	parit; longkang	溝仔
Draw, to (a picture)	tulis	畫
Draw, to (pull)	tarek	拖
Draw near, to	hampir	就近
Draw out, to	chabot	挽
Drawer	lachi	拖
Dream	mimpi	夢
Dress	pakian	衣服
Drink, to	minum	飲
Drive, to (in a carriage)	naik kreta	坐車
Drop, to	jatoh	落
Drop, to let	jatohkan	放落去
Drum	rbana	鼓
Drunk	mabok	酒醉

Dry	kring	乾
Dry, to (in the wind)	anginkan	吹風
Dry, to (in the sun)	jmorkan	曝日
Duck	itek	鴨
Dumb	bisu	啞口
Dust (in a room)	habok	塵埃
Dust (on the road)	dbu	土粉
Dust, to	sapu habok	拂土
Each	masing-masing	各个
Ear	tlinga	耳仔
Early (in the day)	pagi-pagi	早
Earth, the	dunia; bumi	地
Earth (ground)	tanah	土
Earthenware pot	blanga	磁地器
Easily	snang	快
East	timor	東
Easy	snang; mudah	易
Eat, to	makan	食
Edge	tpi	邊
Edge (of knives, etc.)	mata	刀鋩
Egg	tlor	卵

Eight	dlapan	八
Elephant	gajah	象
Eleven	s-blas	十一人
Else, some one	lain orang	別人
Else, anything	lain apa-apa	別物
Else, nothing	lain tidak	也無
Empty	kosong	空
End (finish)	ksudahan	息
End (extremity)	hujong	尾
Enemy	musoh	對敵
England	negri Inggris	大英國
Enjoy, to	suka	欣喜
Enough	chukop	足額
Enquire, to (ask)	tanya	問
Enter, to (go in)	masok	入
Equal	sama	平
Error	salah	錯悮
Escape, to	lari	逃走
Eternal	kkal	永遠
Europe	negri Iropah	歐羅巴國
Evening (after sun-set)	malam	間

Evening (before sunset)	ptang	
Ever	pernah	
Ever, for	s-lama-lama-nya	
Every	masing-masing; tiap-tiap	
Evil	jahat	
Exact	btul	
Examine, to	preksa	
Exchange, to	tukar	
Expense	blanja	
Expensive	mahal	
Extra	lbeh	
Eye	mata	
Face	muka	
Fair (just)	'adil; patut; btul	
False	bohong	
Fall, to	jatoh	
Family	isi rumah	
Fan	kipas	
Far (of distance)	jauh	
Far (much)	banyak	
Fast (quick)	lkas	

Fast (abstinence)	puasa	禁食
Fasten, to	ikat	綁
Fat	gmok	肥
Father	bapa	老父
Fathom (2 yards)	dpa	澗
Fault	salah	過失
Fear, to	takot	驚
Feather	bulu	毛
Feed, to	makan; kasi makan	飼
Feel, to	rasa	摸
Female	prempuan; btina	女 某查
Fence	pagar	籬 笆
Fetch, to	ambil	取
Fever	dmam	熱
Few	sdikit	寡
Field	padang	田 園
Fight, to	berklahi	相打
Fill, to	isikan	倒至滿
Find, to	dapat	尋着
Fine	dnda	罰銀
Fine (not coarse)	halus	幼

Fine (elegant)	bagus	雅
Finger	jari	指頭仔
Finish, to	habis; habiskan	做明白
Fire	api	火
Fire, to (of guns)	tembak	放銃
Fireworks	bunga api	煙火
Firewood	kayu api	柴頭
First pertama, nmber satu *(col)*		起頭一個第一
First, at	mula-mula	
Fish	ikan	魚
Fit (suitable)	patut	好勢
Five	lima	五
Flag	bndera	旗
Flagstaff	tiang-bndera	旗桿
Flat	rata	扁
Flesh	daging	肉
Float, to	timbol	浮
Flood	ayer bah	淹水
Floor	lantai	土脚
Flour	tpong	麵粉
Flower	bunga	花

SINGAPORE TRIGLOT VOCABULARY.

Fly	lalat	蠅
Fly, to	terbang	飛
Fold	lapis	疊
Fold, to	lipat	摺
Follow, to	ikut	趁
Food	makanan	食
Foolish	bodoh	愚
Foot	kaki	脚
For	bagai	替
For (because)	kerna	因爲
Forbid, to	larangkan	禁
Foreigner	orang dagang	外國人
Forget, to	lupa	不記得
Forgive, to	ampunkan; ma'afkan	赦免
Fork	garfu	鎝仔
Form	rupa	樣
Former	dhulu	早先
Formerly	dhulu	在却
Forsake, to	tinggalkan	放
Fortnight	dua minggo	二禮拜
Four	ampat	四

Fowl	ayam	鷄
Free	bibas; merdheka	自由
Friend	kawan	朋友
Frog	katak; kodok	田蛤仔
From (places)	deri	對頭
From (a person)	deripada	對
Front, in	di-hadapan	前
Fruit	buah	菓子
Fry	goring	煎
Fulfil, to	sampaikan; gnapi	應驗
Full	pnoh	滿
Further	lbeh jauh	較遠
Game	permainan	遊戲
Gamble	main judi	賭博
Gaol	pnjara; jeil	監舘
Garden	kbun	花園
Gardener	tukang-kbun	園丁
Gate	pintu	門
Gather, to (pick up)	pungut	挽收
Gather together, to	kumpol; kampongkan	先
Gentleman	tuan	生

Get, to	dapat	得着
Get up, to	bangun; bangkit	起來
Ghost	hantu	鬼怪
Gift	hadia; pmbrian	送、賞賜
Girl	anak-prempuan	查某孩子
Give, to	kasi; bri	俾送
Give back, to	kasi pulang	還
Glad	suka-hati	歡喜
Glass (mirror)	chermin muka	面鏡
Glass (for drinking)	glas	杯
Glorious	mulia	榮顯
Glory	kmulia'an	榮光
Glue	perkat	膠
Goat	kambing	山羊
God	Allah	上帝
Gold	'mas	金
Go, to	pergi	去
Go on, to (start)	jalan	行
Go in, to	masok	入
Go home, to	pulang	到去
Go down, to	turun	落去

Go up, to	naik	上
Good	baik	好
Good, no	ta'guna	無用
Good, what is the	apa guna	甚麽用
Good-bye	tabek	請
Goods	barang-barang	貨物
Gospel	Injil	福音
Grace	anugrah	恩典
Grand	bsar	大
Grand-child	chuchu	孫
Grand-father	nenek; dato'	公公; 外公
Grand-mother	nenek prempuan	媽媽; 外媽
Grass	rumput	草
Grave	kubur	墓
Gravy	kuah	茄色
Great	bsar	大
Great deal, a	banyak	盡多
Green	hijau	青
Grief	susah	煩惱
Grind, to	kisar; giling	挾
Ground	tanah	土

Grow, to (as plants)	tumboh	愈大
Grow, to (increase)	tambah	加添
Grow, to (become)	mnjadi	生.做
Gruel	kanji	泔糜
Grumble, to	bersungut	雜雜念
Guess, to	agak	量約
Guide, to	pimpin	引
Guilty	salah; berdosa	有罪
Gun	snapang	銃
Habit	'adat	風俗
Hair	bulu	毛
Hair (of the head)	rambot	頭毛
Half	s-tngah; s-paruh	一半
Hammer	pmukol bsi	鎚
Hand	tangan	手
Hand-cart	kreta tarek	人車
Handwriting	tulisan; khat	筆跡
Handkerchief	sapu-tangan	手巾
Handle (of doors, &c.)	tangan	柄
Hang, to	gantong; gantongkan	掛
Happen, to	jadi	成

Happy	snang	有福氣
Hard	kras	硬
Harm (damage)	bnchana; chlaka	害
Harm, no	tidak salah	無害着
Harness	pakian kuda	背馬不
Haste	lkas	緊緊
Hat	topi	帽
Hatchet	kapak	斧
Hate, to	bnchi	怨恨
Have, to	ada; beroleh	有
Head	kpala	頭頭
Headache	sakit-kpala	醫殼殼病
Heal, to	sumboh	勇好
Health	sehat	聽健
Hear, to	dngar	心
Heart	hati	熱
Heat	panas	天天堂
Heaven	shorga	上
Heavens, the (sky)	langit	重
Heavy	brat	籬笆
Hedge	pagar	

He, him, she, her	dia; ia	伊
Help, to	tolong	帮助
Hell	nraka	地獄
Hen	ayam btina	鷄母
Here	sini; di-sini	在此
Here (hither)	k-mari	來此
Hide, to	smbunyikan	匿密藏
High	tinggi	高
Hill	bukit	山
Hire, to (things)	sewa	稅
Hire, to (labour)	upah	倩
His, hers	dia punya	伊的
History	hikayat	記略
Hit, to (strike)	pukol	打
Hit, to (a mark)	kna	撞
Hoe	changkol	鋤
Hoist, to	angkat	升
Hold, to	pgang	貯
Hold, to (contain)	isi; muat	盛
Hole	lobang	空穿
Holiday	hari lpas.	閒日

Holy	suchi	聖
Home	rumah	厝
Home, at	di-rumah	在厝
Honest	tulus	忠
Honour (greatness)	kmulia'an	榮尊仰
Honour (respect)	hormat	的厚顯敬望
Hope, to	harap	望
Horn	tandoh	角
Horse	kuda	馬
Hot (of fire)	panas	燒
Hot (of spices)	pdas	辣
Hotel	rumah tumpangan	客館
Hour	jam	點鐘
House	rumah	厝宅
How	bgimana	將若何
How often	brapa kali	幾次
How long	brapa lama	若久
How much	brapa	幾干
How much (of price)	brapa herga	若價錢
Humble	rndah	謙遜
Hundred, one	s-ratus	一百

Hungry	lapar	饑
Hurt, to (wound)	luka	傷
Husband	laki	丈夫
Hush!	diam	靜靜
Hut	pondok	寮仔
I	sahia ; aku	我
Ice	ayer-batu	霜
Idle	malas	懶惰
Idol	berhala	偶像
If	kalau ; jika	設使
Ignorant	bbal	酣慢
Ill	sakit	破病
Immediately	skarang ini ; lkas	隨時
Important	brat	要緊
Impossible	yang ta'boleh jadi ; mstahil	不能
Improve, to	mmbaiki	創較好
In	dalam	在內
In (inside)	di-dalam	如面
In order that	spaya	是
Inch	jari ; inchi	寸
Included, to be	masok	包內在

SINGAPORE TRIGLOT VOCABULARY. 45

Inconvenient	ta'snang	不便
Incorrect	salah	不着
Increase, to	tambah; tambahkan	加添
Indeed	s-bnar-nya	眞正
Index	isi kitab; fihrist	目錄
India	negri Hindi	印度國
India-rubber	gtah	樹乳
Industrious	rajin	急計
Inform, to	bri tau	通知
Ink	tinta; dawat	墨水
Inkstand	tmpat-tinta	墨水罐
Inquire, to	tanya; preksa	問
Inside	di-dalam	內面
Inspect, to	preksa	查考
Instead of	ganti	替
Intend, to	mau; hndak	要
Interpreter	juru-bhasa	通事
Into	k-dalam	內
Invite, to	jmpot	請
Iron	bsi	鐵
Is	ada	是呢

Is not	bukan	不是
Island	pulau	海嶼
It	dia ; itu	伊
Itself	sndiri	自脚
Jail	pnjara	監拘
Japan	negri Jpon	日本國
Java	negri Jawa	吧嚕
Jealous	chmburu	怨妒
Jesus	Isa	耶穌
Jew	orang Yahudi	猶太人
Join, to	hubong ; sambong	合連結
Joy	ksuka'an	快樂
Judge	hakim	色視
Judge, to	hukumkan	審判
Judge, to (consider)	timbang	嫌
Jump, to	lompat	跳
Juice	ayer-buah	汁
Just (righteous)	'adil ; bnar	公道
Just (just now)	tadi ; bharu	當今
Just gone out	bharu kluar	當今出門
Keep, to (retain)	simpan	收

Keep, to (preserve)	plihara	庇照 佑
Keep, to (a promise)	sampaikan	約
Keep, to (dogs, horses)	pliharakan	飼鎖返足刣刣刣號有王國吻灶風跪刀菜打結
Key	anak kunchi; kunchi (col)	匙
Kick, to (backwards)	tndang	攆
Kick, to (forwards)	sepak	攆死
Kill, to	bunoh	死
Kill (for food with religious rites)	smbleh	
Kill, to (fowls etc)	potong	
Kind (sort)	macham; jnis	欸
Kind (amiable)	berkasihan	愛仁
King	raja	王 帝
Kingdom	kraja'an	
Kiss, to	chium	
Kitchen	dapur	
Kite	layang-layang	脚
Kneel, to	berlutut; bertlut	吹
Knife	pisau	
Knife (chopping)	parang	刀
Knock, to	ktok	
Knot	simpul	頭

Know, to	tau	知識
Know, to (be acquainted with)	knal	不少
Know, I dont	ntah	知
Lad	orang muda	年
Ladder	tangga	梯
Lake	tasek	湖
Lamb	anak-domba	羊
Lame	tempang	跛
Lamp	plita; lampu (col)	燈
Land	tanah	地
Language	bhasa	話
Large	bsar	大
Last	pnghabisan; akhir	路
Last, to	tahan; tinggal	久
Last night	s-malam	昨
Last year	tahun lalu	舊
Late	lambat	晏
Lately	tadi; bharu	近
Laugh, to	tertawa	笑
Laugh at, to	tertawakan	耻笑
Law	hukum; undang-undang	律法

Law of Moses	Taurit	摩西五經
Lawyer	wakil	狀師
Lay, to (place)	taroh	置
Lazy	malas	懶惰
Lead	timah hitam	鉛
Lead, to	pimpin	引
Leaf	daun	葉
Leaf (of paper)	hlai	頁
Leaky	bochor	漏
Learn, to	blajar	學
Leather	kulit	皮
Leave, to	tinggalkan	離開
Leave off, to	berhenti	煞
Left	kiri	左旁
Leg	kaki	腿
Lend, to	pinjamkan	借人
Length	panjang	長
Leper	orang sakit kusta	癩疾的
Less	kurang	較少
Lesson	plajaran	工課
Lest	spaya jangan	驚了

Let, to (allow)	biar	准
Let, to (for hire)	sewa	稅
Let go, to	lpas	放
Letter	surat	批
Letter (character)	huruf	字
Level	rata	平
Lid	tutopan; tudongan	蓋
Lie, a	bohong	賊 白
Lie down, to	baring	臥
Life	hidop; haiat	命 性
Lift, to	angkat	來 起 扶
Light	trang	光
Light (daylight)	siang	時 日
Light (in weight)	ringan	輕
Light, to	pasang	點
Lighter (barge)	tongkang	舩 大
Lightning	kilat	閃 電
Like	sperti; s-rupa	似 相愛如
Like, to	suka	
Like that	bgitu	是 若
Like this	bgini	此

Lime (fruit)	limau nipis	桔仔
Lime (mineral)	kapur	灰
Line	baris	痕
Lining	alas; lapis	裏
Lion	singa	獅
Lip	bibir	嘴唇
Liquid	chaer	流形
Listen, to	dngar	聽
Little (small)	kchil	細
Little, a	s-dikit	寡
Live, to (dwell)	tinggal	住
Loaf of bread, a	s-biji roti	麵包
Lock	kunchi	鎖
Lock, to	kunchikan	鎖
Lodge, to	tumpang	宿
Lonely	sunyi	無
Long (measure)	panjang	長
Long (time)	lama	久
Look at, to	tengo'; pandang	看
Look for, to	chari	尋
Loose	longgar	另

Lord (God)	Tuhan
Lord (master)	tuan
Lose, to	hilang
Lose, to (incur loss)	rugi
Loud	kwat; nyaring
Love	kaseh; chinta *(col)*
Love, to	kasihi
Low	rndah
Lower, to	turunkan
Mad	gila
Madam	mem
Maggot	ulat
Make, to	buat; bikin *(col)*
Make known, to	kasi tau; khabarkan
Make out, to	mngerti
Malay	Mlayu
Male	jantan
Man (individuals)	orang
Man (mankind)	manusia
Manage, to (affairs)	jalankan
Manage, to (succeed)	tau; dapat

Mango	buah mangga	樣仔
Mangusteen	buah manggis	網訖
Manner (kind)	macham	樣式
Manner (behaviour)	klakuan	欵
Many	banyak	多
Many, how	brapa	若干
Map	pta	地圖
Mark	tanda	號
Market	pasar	街市
Marriage	kahwin	婚姻
Marry, to	berkahwin	娶妻
Mast	tiang	桅
Master	tuan	頭家
Mat	tikar	蓆
Mat (for covering)	kajang	
Match	korek api	火柴
Matter (affair)	perkara	事務
Matter, what is the?	apa salah	甚麽事
Mattress	tilam	褥仔
May	boleh	可、能
May be; it may be	barangkali	或者

Me	sahia	我
Mean, to (intend)	mau; hndak	想欲
Meaning	arti	意思
Measure, to (length)	ukor	度
Measure, to (capacity)	sukatkan	量
Meat	daging	肉
Medicine	obat	藥
Meek	lmbot-hati	溫柔
Meet, to	jumpa	遇着
Meet together, to	berkumpol	聚集
Meeting	kumpolan	相會
Mend, to	mmbaiki	補
Mercy	kasihan; rahmat	慈悲
Midday	tngah hari	日午
Middle	tngah	中
Middle, in the	tngah-tngah; sama tngah	中央
Midnight	tngah-malam	夜半
Midst	tngah	中央
Might	boleh	能
Mile	batu	里
Milk	susu	乳

Mind, to (care)	fduli	要細憶念無我分打錯摻目額鐳猿天月月更早平
Mind, to (beware)	jaga	緊貳得頭相个
Mind, to (think of)	ingat	
Mind, the	'akal	
Mind, never	tidak apa	千
Mine	sahia punya	
Minute	minit; sa'at	
Miss, to	ta'kna	至無
Mistake	salah	快
Mix, to	champur	
Moment, a	s-kjap	久瞬
Money	wang	
Money (copper)	duit	
Monkey	munyit	
Monsoon	musim	時
Month	bulan	
Moon	bulan	
Moonlight	bulan trang	光
More	lbeh; lagi	多更 、
Morning	pagi	起
Morning, good	tabek	安

Mosquito	nyamok	蚊
Mosquito net	klambu	蚊帳
Most	yang terlbeh	第一多
Mother	mak; ibu; bonda	老母
Motive	sbab	緣故
Mountain	gunong	山
Mouse	tikus	老鼠 仔
Mouth	mulut	口
Move, to	bergrak; grakkan	震搬動
Move, to (remove)	pindah; pindahkan	頭退去
Move back, to	undor	頭後
Mr.	tuan	多家
Mrs.	mem	娘家
Much	banyak	多
Much, how	brapa	若麽
Mud	lumpur	刣泥
Murder, to	bunoh	樂死
Music	bunyi-bunyian	應音
Must	msti; harus	該
Mutton	daging kambing	羊肉
My	sahia punya	我个

Nail	paku	釘
Nail (finger)	kuku	指甲
Naked	tlanjang	赤體
Name	nama	名
Name, to	namakan; glarkan	名號就起
Namely	ia'itu	名是
Narrate, to	chertrakan	講
Narrow	smpet	狹
Nation	bangsa	國
Naughty	nakal; jahat	歹
Near	dkat	近
Nearly	hampir; dkat	差
Neck	lehir	領
Need, to	mau	欲
Need not	ta'usah	不用
Needle	jarom	針
Neglect, to	lalai	不理
Nest	sarang	巢
Net (casting)	jala	網
Net (drag)	pukat	網
Never	ta'pernah	未曾

Never yet	blum pernah	未有
New	bharu	新新
News	khabar	消息
Newspaper	surat khabar	新聞紙
Next (in place)	dkat; s-blah	隔壁
Next (after)	kmdian	然後
Next month	lain bulan	後月
Nice	sdap	巧味
Night	malam	瞑
Night, To-	ini malam	今夜
Night, last	s-malam	昨晚
Night, all	s-panjang malam	全夜
Nine	smbilan	九
No	tidak	無
No one	tiada s'orang; s'orang-pun tidak	半人
Noise	bunyi	聲
Noon	tngah-hari	午日
North	utara	北
Nose	hidong	鼻
Not	bukan; tidak	不是、
Not, do	jangan	不可

SINGAPORE TRIGLOT VOCABULARY.

Not, is	bukan; tiada	不是
Not yet	blum	尚未
Nothing	tiada apa	無物
Nothing else	lain tidak	也無
Now	skarang	當今
Now and then	kadang-kadang	三五時
Number	angka; nombor (col)	數
Oar	daiung	漿
Oath	sumpah	咒誓
Oath, to take an	bersumpah	發誓願
Obey, to	turut; ikut (col)	順
Ocean	lautan	洋
O'clock	pukol	點鐘
Of (possessive)	punya	之
Of (out of, consisting of)	deripada	對自
Of course	psti	對然
Off	deri	去
Off, to be	pergi	息
Off, to leave	berhenti	寫捷
Office	ofis; gdong (col)	字樓
Often	slalu; banyak kali	捷捷

Often, how	brapa kali	幾次
Oil	minyak	油
Oil (mineral)	minyak tanah	土油
Old, how (age)	brapa umor	幾歲
Old	lama	舊
Old (of age)	tua	老
On	atas; di-atas	頂面
On to	k-atas	頂
Once	s-kali	一次
One	satu or s-	一
One by one	satu-satu	一个一个
Oneself	diri-nya	本身
Onion	bawang	葱
Only	sahaja	不過了
Open	terbuka	開
Open, to	buka	開
Openly	nyata	顯然
Opinion	fikiran; sangka	意見
Opium, to smoke	makan chandu	食鴉片
Or	atau	或是
Orange	limau manis	柑

Order, to (command)	suroh; psan	吩咐
Order, to (commission)	psan	拜托
Order (arrangement)	aturan	次序
Order (command)	hukum	命令
Order that, in	spaya	若此
Other	lain	别个
Ought	patut; harus	應該
Our	kita punya	咱的
Out	luar; di-luar; k-luar	外面
Out, to go	kluar	出去
Out, to go (as fire)	padam	灰
Outside	di-luar	外面
Oven	dapur	火爐
Over (above)	atas; di-atas; k-atas	頂面
Over (finished)	sudah	明白
Over (surplus)	lbeh	有餘
Owe, to	berhutang	欠債
Own	sndiri punya	自己
Own, to (possess)	mmpunya'i; beroleh	有管
Own, to (confess)	mngaku	認
Ox	lmbu jantan	牛公

Pack up, to (a parcel)	bungkuskan	包
Padlock	kunchi mangga	鎖
Page (of a book)	muka	頁
Pail	timba; tong	桶
Pain	sakit	痛
Painful	sakit	能痛
Paint	chat	油漆
Paint, to	sapu chat	拭漆
Pair, a	satu pasang	一雙
Paper	kertas	紙
Parafin	minyak tanah	土油
Parcel	bungkus	包炭
Pardon	ampun; ma'af	赦罪
Pardon, to	ampunkan; ma'afkan	赦免
Parents	mak-bapa	父母
Part	bhagian	一塊
Partly	s-paroh	有個
Pass, to	lalu	過
Past	sudah; sudah lalu	過了
Paste	perkat	糊
Patch	tampal	補

旁

Patient	sabar	忍耐
Pattern	chontoh	樣工
Pay	gaji	還錢
Pay, to	bayar	無還
Pay, it does not	tiada untong	錢
Peace (of mind)	sntausa	太平趁安
Peace (from fighting)	damai	處平和
Peace, to make	damaikan orang	眞和
Pearl	mutiara	珠
Pen	kalam	筆
Pencil	patlut	鉛筆
Penitent	bertaubat	反悔
Penknife	pisau lipat; pisau kchil	刀仔
People	orang-orang	百姓
Pepper	lada	胡椒
Perfect	smporna	齊全
Perform, to	lakukan	成做
Perhaps	barangkali	或是
Perish, to	binasa	沉倫
Persecute, to	aniayakan	窘迫
Person, a	s'orang	一人

Persuade, to	pujokkan	勸
Pick up, to	pungut	拾
Picture	gamber	相影
Piece, a	s-kping	一塊
Pig	babi	猪
Pigeon	merpati	鴿仔
Pillow	bantal	枕頭
Pillow case	sarong bantal	枕頭袋
Pin	pniti *(col)*	針
Pineapple	nanas	梨
Pipe	panchuran	溝
Pitch	damar	鼎馬油
Pity	kasihan	憫憐
Pity, to	sayangkan	憐可
Place	tmpat	所在
Place of, in	ganti	替
Place, to	taroh; buboh	落
Plain (clear)	trang; nyata	明
Plain (clear ground)	padang	平埔
Plan (method)	jalan	法度
Plane	ktam	刨刀

Plank	papan	枋
Plant, to	tanam	栽
Plant, a	poko'; tanaman	樹仔
Plate	piring; pinggan	盤
Play, to	main-main	耍玩意
Pleasant	snang; sdap	中意八樂
Please, to	sukakan; perknankan 喜歡	俾決盛
Pleasure	ksuka'an	豐仔
Plenty	banyak	袋
Pocket	kochek; saku	詩
Poem	sha'ir	尾
Point (end)	hujong	海
Point (of land)	tanjong	角指
Point, to	tunjok	毒
Poison	rachun	毒
Poisonous	bisa	一
Pole	batang	枝查
Policeman	mata-mata	街小
Pony	kuda kchil	馬貧
Poor	mskin	窮有
Possess, to	mmpunya'i; beroleh	

Possible	boleh	能
Pot (earthenware)	blanga	砂
Potato	ubi bnggala; ubi *(col)*	蕃薯
Pour, to	tuang	倒出
Power	kuasa	權
Practise, to	blajar; biasakan diri	學習
Praise, to	puji	讚美
Prawn	udang	蝦
Pray, to	minta do'a	求
Prayer	do'a; perminta'an	祈禱
Preach, to	khabarkan	講道理
Precious	indah	寶貝
Prefer, to	suka lbeh	較愛
Prepare, to	sdiakan; siapkan	備辦
Present, a	hadia; pmbrian	送個物
Present, to	kasi; bri	送的
Present, to be	ada; hadlir	在
Present, at	skarang	現在
Presently	lagi s-kjap	霎時、
Press, to	tkan; apit	假夾
Pretend, to	buat-buat	映

Pretty	chantek; elok	美
Prevent, to	tgahkan	阻擋
Price	herga	價錢
Prick, to	tikam	鑒着
Priest	imam	祭司
Prince	anak raja	太子
Print, to	chap; chapkan	印
Printed	terchap	印
Prison	pnjara	監
Prisoner	orang salah	監囚
Profess, to	mngaku	認
Profit	untong	得利
Promise	janji; perjanjian	應許
Promise, to	berjanji	搭應
Pronounce, to	bunyikan	講音
Proper	patut	好勢
Property	herta-bnda	家業
Prophet	nabi	先知
Prosecute, to	da'wa	訟
Protect, to	pliharakan; lindongkan	佑庇、護保
Proud	sumbong	傲驕

Prove, to	trangkan; nyatakan	出 憑 據
Psalms, the	Mzmur; Zabur	詩篇
Pudding	kweh	餅粿、
Pull, to	tarek	拖
Pull out, to	chabot	拔
Pump	bomba	水
Punish, to	hukumkan; seksakan	刑 刑罰 抽罰
Punishment	hukuman; seksa	學 刑罰
Pupil (learner)	murid	清 生
Pure (clean)	suchi	特 氣
Purpose, on	dngan sngaja	腰 故意
Purse	pundi-pundi	推 包
Push, to	tolak	置
Put, to	taroh	置 在
Put in, to	masokkan	穿 內
Put on, to (clothes)	pakai	灰
Put out, to (fire)	padamkan	園
Put together, to	pasang	多
Quantity	banyak	寃
Quarrel, to	berbantah; bersliseh	相 家
Quarrel, to (fight)	berklahi	爭

Quarter	suku	一份 四
Question, a	sual	間
Quick	lkas	緊活
Quick lime	kapur tohor	緊灰 靜俱
Quiet	diam	靜女
Quite	s-kali; s-kali-kali	皆闈
Queen	raja prempuan	王雨
Race, a	lumba	走扶
Rain	hujan	竪
Raise, to (lift)	angkat	起使
Raise, to (set up)	berdirikan	立設葡
Raise from the dead, to	{ bangkitkan deri-pada mati }	活復罕
Raisins	buah anggor	乾併鳥
Rarely	jarang	葡少
Rat	tikus	得更
Rather (somewhat)	sdikit	鼠籐
Rather (in preference)	lbeh suka	許剌
Rattan	rotan	愛到
Razor	pisau chukor	刀頭讀
Reach, to	sampai	
Read, to	bacha	

Read the Kora'an	mngaji	讀咕嘞
Ready	sdia; siap	便辦
Ready, to make or get	sdiakan; siapkan	備
Real	btul; bnar	真在
Really	s-bnar-nya	實
Reap, to	tuai	收刈
Reason	sbab; fasal	緣故
Rebel, to	derhaka	背叛
Receipt	rsit	收單
Receive, to	trima	受
Recover, to (health)	mnjadi sumboh	再健康
Recover, to (get back)	dapat kmbali	再得着
Red	merah	紅
Redeem, to (from slavery)	tbuskan	贖囘
Reed	buloh	蘆竹
Refuse, to	enggan	不理
Reign, to	jadi raja; pgang prentah	治
Reins	ras	馬索
Reject, to	tolakkan; buangkan	棄絕
Rejoice, to	bersuka-suka; bergmar	歡喜
Relation	saudara	親戚

Religion	agama	教
Remain, to (stay)	tinggal; berhenti	住等
Remain, to (wait)	nanti	待
Remain, to (left over)	tinggal	伸
Remember, to	ingat	記
Remind, to	bri ingat	指
Remove, to	pindah; pindahkan	搬
Remove, to (take away)	bawa pergi	携 得 點去 去
Renew, to	bharui	重新
Rent	sewa	稅
Repair, to	baiki	收理
Repeat, to	kata kmbali	再講
Repent, to	bertaubat; ssal	悔改
Repentance	taubat	悔改
Reply, to	jawab	答
Request, a	perminta'an	求 情
Request, to	minta	懇求
Require, to	mau; berkahandak	歉用
Rescue, to	lpaskan	救
Resist, to	lawan	抵當
Respect, to	hormat	敬

Rest	perhentian	息
Rest, the	yang tinggal; yang lbeh	伸個結復
Result	yang jadi deripada	局結到
Resurrection	kbangkitan	活去還
Return, to (go back)	balik; pulang	報
Return, to (give back)	pulangkan	報
Return, to (reward)	balaskan	答粟
Reward	upah; fhalla	賞米
Rice (in the husk)	padi	飯
Rice (husked)	bras	富
Rice (boiled)	nasi	錢
Rich	kaya	騎
Riches	kkaya'an	右
Ride, to	tunggang kuda	公
Right (side)	kanan	着義
Right (proper)	patut	手
Right (correct)	btul	熟
Righteous	bnar	財起
Ring	chinchin	馬指
Ripe	masak	平
Rise, to (get up)	bangun; bangkit	平來

Rise, to (go up)	naik	上水
River	sungai	溪
Road	jalan	路
Robber	pnchuri	盜
Rock	batu	石
Roll, to	guling; golek	誤
Roll up, to	gulong	卷
Roof	atap	塔 亞蓋
Roof (tiled)	atap gnting	厝
Room (space)	tmpat	所 任
Room, a	bilek	房
Root	akar	根
Rope	tali bsar	大 索
Rotten (putrid)	busok	朽 爛
Rotten (worn out)	burok	朽 爛
Rough	kasar	粗 俗
Round	bulat	圓
Round (around)	kliling	四 處
Rouse, to	bangunkan	醒
Row, to	berdaiung	撾
Row (line)	baris	一 畷

Row (disturbance)	gadoh	相攪 爭攪
Row (noise)	bising	磨糞
Rub, to	gosok	舵
Rubbish	sampah	粗
Rudder	kmudi	滅治
Rude	kasar	規隔 掃
Ruin, to	binasakan	
Rule, to	prentahkan	亡珥
Rule, a (order)	hukum	矩
Rule, a (measuring)	kayu ukor	尺
Run, to	lari	走
Rust	karat	銹
Sack	karong; saku	袋
Sacrifice	korban	祭 祀
Sad	susah-hati; brat-hati	憂 悶
Safe	slamat	穩
Sago	sagu	謝 米
Sail, a	layer	篷
Sail, to	blayer	駛篷
Sailor	anak-prahu; khlasi	水手
Salary	gaji	束金

Sale (auction)	lelong	喝龍桼
Salt	garam	鹽
Salt (in taste)	masin	鹹
Salvation	slamat	救
Same	sama	同
Same, all the	sama juga	同相
Sample	chonto	辦貨
Sand	pasir	沙
Sandals	trompa	鞋木
Satan	Shaitan; Iblis	但撒
Satisfied	puas-hati	足知
Sauce	kuah	湯
Savage	garang	雄
Save, to (from danger)	slamatkan; lpaskan	亞救
Save, to (protect)	lindongkan; pliharakan	佑庇
Save, to (as money)	simpan	收
Saw	gergaji	仔鋸
Say, to	kata; katakan	講
Scarce	jarang	有罕
School	skola	堂學
Science	elmu	學

Scissors	gunting	剪刀
Scream, to	bertriak	喉呼
Sea, the	laut	海
Search, to (look for)	chari	尋
Search, to (examine)	preksa	勘窮
Season	musim	天時
Seat	tmpat-dudok	坐位
Second	yang k-dua; nombor dua	第二
Secret, a	rahsia	機蜜
Secret; secretly	tersmbunyi	暗靜
Security (bail)	jamin	擔認
See, to	nampak; lihat	看
See to, to	jaga	顧
Seed	biji	種子
Seek, to	chari	尋
Seem, to	nampak	相似
Seemingly	rupa-nya	恍惚
Seize, to	tangkap; pgang	擎得擒
Seldom	jarang	罕
Self	diri	自已
Sell, to	jual	賣

Send, to	kirim; hantar	寄差
Send for, to (persons)	panggil	叫伊來
Send for, to (things)	psan	叫伊取
Sense (meaning)	arti	意思
Sense (intelligence)	pngertian; 'akal	智識
Sentence (judgment)	hukum	判斷
Separate, to	chraikan	分離
Separate, to (divide)	blahkan	分開
Separate, to (set apart)	asingkan; sndirikan	單摘
Serious (important)	brat	傷重
Set, to	taroh	放
Set, to (of the sun)	turun	落
Set up, to	berdirikan	設立着
Settle, to (a quarrel)	slsaikan	定
Seven	tujoh	七
Several	bbrapa	幾個若
Sew, to	jait	縫
Shade	nawang	影
Shadow	bayang	影
Shafts (of a carriage)	bom	柄
Shake, to	goyangkan; kbaskan	搖

Shake hands, to	jabat tangan	純手
Shaky	longgar	無緊
Shall	nanti	要
Shallow	tohor	淺
Sham, to	buat-buat	假
Shame	malu	貝 影
Shape	rupa	欵 誚
Share, a	bhagian	份 樣
Share, to	bhagikan	分
Sharp	tajam	利
Sharpen, to	tajamkan; asahkan	磨
Shave, to	chukor	剃
She	dia; ia	伊
Shed	bangsal	草
Sheep	domba; kambing (col)	羊
Sheet (for a bed)	slimut	被 厝
Sheet (of paper)	hlai	張 單
Shell (of fish)	siput	殼
Shelter, to	lindongkan	遮
Shepherd	gmbala	牧者
Shew, to	tunjok; unjok	顯明

Shift, to	pindahkan	徙
Shine, to	berchahia	照
Ship	kapal	船
Ship of war	kapal prang	船戰
Shirt	kmeja	衫短
Shoe	kasut	鞋
Shoot, to	tembak	銃打
Shop	kdai	店
Shore	pantai	墩海
Short	pendek	短
Short (deficient)	kurang	足不
Shoulder	bahu	頭肩
Shout, to	bertriak; bersru	喝
Shove, to	tolak	推
Show, to (point out)	tunjok; unjok	示指
Show, to (prove)	nyatakan	明創
Shower	hujan	雨
Shrink, to (grow small)	kerut	虬
Shut, to	tutop	關
Shy	takot	人畏
Sick	sakit	痛破

Sick, to be (vomit)	muntah	吐
Sickness	pnyakit	痛
Side	s-blah	邊
Side, this	s-blah sini	此邊
Sieve	nyiru	篩
Sign	tanda	記號
Sign, to	taroh tanda tangan; sain (col)	落名
Silent	diam	靜
Silk	sutra	絲
Silly	bodoh	愚戇
Silver	perak	銀
Similar	s-rupa	相同
Sin	dosa	罪
Since	sminjak; deripada waktu	既然、吟
Sing, to	nyanyi	唱
Sink, to	tngglam	沉
Sink, to (founder)	karam	沉
Sir	tuan	先生
Sister	saudara prempuan	姊妹
Sister, elder	kakak	大姊
Sister, younger	adek prempuan	小妹

Sister-in-law	ipar prempuan	大姨
Sit, to	dudok	坐
Six	anam	六
Size	bsar	大
Skin	kulit	皮
Sky, the	langit	蒼穹 天、
Slanting	chundrong; mering	斜抉
Slap, to	tmpar; tmpeling	塗刮
Slate	papan loh	盤臥
Slave	hamba	僕奴
Slay, to	bunoh	死踏
Sleep, to	tidor	顛滑
Slip, to	glinchir	滑慢
Slippery	lichin	慢慢
Slow	lambat	慢
Slowly	perlahan-lahan; plan-plan (co.)	慢狡
Sly	cherdek	怪小
Small	kchil	痘
Small-pox	chachar	打
Smash, to	hanchorkan	碎碎
Smell, a	bau	味

Smell, to	chium	鼻抹烟
Smile, to	snyium	笑吻
Smoke	asap	食烟
Smoke, to (tobacco)	hisap roko'	食烟
Smoke opium, to	hisap chandu	片鴉
Smooth	lichin	平
Snake	ular	蛇
Snatch, to	rbot	揀
So	bgitu; itu macham	如此如
So that	spaya	生此
Soak, to	rndam; rndamkan	浸
Soap	sabon	雪文
Soft	lmbot; lmbek	軟
Soil, the	tanah	土
Soil, to	kotorkan	穢污染
Soldier	soldado	兵
Sole (only)	sahaja	單孤
Sole of the foot	tapak kaki	底跡脚
Some	sdikit	小可
Some one	s'orang	有人
Something	satu barang; satu perkara	有物

Sometimes	kadang-kadang	有的罕
Son	anak laki-laki	的男子
Son-in-law	mnantu	子婿
Song	nyanyi; lagu	歌臨痛憂
Soon	lkas; lagi s-kjap	邊心
Sore	sakit	問號
Sorrow	duka; ksusahan	悶
Sorry	susah-hati; brat-hati	苦肝
Sort	macham; jnis	排
Sort, to (arrange)	aturkan	列靈
Soul	nyawa; jiwa	魂聲做
Sound, a	bunyi	湯
Sound, to	berbunyi	聲酸
Soup	kuah; sup (col)	源
Sour (as acids)	asam	頭南
Source	asal	隔
South	slatan	猪位
Sow, a	babi btina	母播
Sow, to	tabor biji	種
Space (room)	tmpat	縫一
Space (interval)	jarak	

Span, a	s-jngkal	一掠
Spark	bunga api	火花
Sparrow	burong pipit	雀鳥仔
Speak, to	chakap	講話
Specimen	chonto	辦頭
Spectacles	chermin mata	目鏡
Speed	lkas	緊
Spell, to	heja	鬥字
Spend, to	blanjakan	開費
Spices	rmpah-rmpah	香料
Spider	laba-laba	蜘蛛
Spill, to	tumpah	倒出
Spin, to	pintal	誤
Spin a top, to	main gasing	釘鹿干
Spirit, a	hantu; jin	怪神
Spirit (of a man)	roh	神
Spirit, The Holy	Roh Allah; Roh-al-kudus	聖神
Spirit (alcohol)	arak	酒
Spit, to	ludah	唾涎
Splendid	elok	燦爛
Split, to	blah; blahkan	破裂

Spoil, to	rosakkan
Sponge	bunga karang
Spoon	sendok; sudu
Sport	permainan
Spot (place)	tmpat
Spot (mark)	tanda; titek
Spout	panchoran
Spread, to (stretch out)	hampar
Spread out, to (expand, open out)	kmbang
Spring (of water)	mata ayer
Spring, to (jump)	lompat
Spy, to	intai; mnyulu
Square	ampat persagi
Squat, to	berjungkok
Squeeze, to	tkan; apit
Stab, to	tikam
Stable (for cattle)	kandang
Stable (for horses)	bangsal kuda
Stain	choring
Stairs	tangga
Stale	lama; basi

Stamp, to (with the feet)	pijak; injak	脚頓印
Stamp, to (impress)	chapkan	堅
Stand, to	berdiri	忍
Stand, to (bear, undergo)	tahan	耐 星粉
Star	bintang	起
Starch	kanji	漿欵
Start, to	jalan	身講
State (condition)	hal	式偽
State, to	kata; katakan	等
Station, police	rumah pasong	厝踏宿
Stay, to (wait)	nanti	待寓
Stay, to (remain)	tinggal	代
Stay, to (lodge)	tumpang	在
Stead of, in	ganti	在偷
Steady	ttap	取火
Steal, to	churi	烟火
Steam	hwap	船鋼
Steamer	kapal api	百
Steel	baja	鎚四楼
Steelyard	daching	舵
Steer, to	pgang kmudi	

Step, a	langkah	步
Stick, a	kayu	木杖仔
Stick, walking	tongkat	杖仔
Stick, to (adhere)	lkat	粘
Stick, to (get entangled)	sangkot	粘條
Stick in, to	chachak	刺
Stick on, to	tampalkan	貼
Stiff	kaku	硬
Still (quiet)	diam	靜
Still (yet)	lagi	尚久
Sting (of insects)	sngat	釘
Stink	bau busok	嗅味
Stir, to (move)	bergrak	震動
Stir up, to	kachaukan	激
Stocking	sarong kaki	袜
Stomach	prot	腹肚
Stone	batu	石
Stool	bangku; krusi	校椅
Stoop, to	tundok	向落
Stop, to (close)	tutop	塞
Storm	ribot	大風

Story	cherita	古
Stout	gmok	肥
Straight	lurus; btul	直
Strange	hairan	奇
Stranger	orang dagang	人
Strap	tali kulit	皮
Stray, to	ssat	迷
Stream (river)	sungai	河
Stream (current)	arus	流
Street	jalan	街
Strength	kkuatan	氣拔力緊
Stretch, to (by pulling)	rgangkan	伸
Stretch, to (lengthen)	panjangkan	創長
Stretch, to (enlarge)	lebarkan; bsarkan	打大
Strike, to	pukol	索
String	tali	踊
Strong	kuat	學健
Study, to	blajer	習
Stupid	bodoh	咸萬
Substitute	ganti	代
Such	dmkian; itu macham	彼號

Suck, to	hisap	吮
Suddenly	tiba-tiba	忽然
Suffer, to	kna susah	受苦
Sugar	gula	糖
Sugar-cane	tbu	甘蔗
Summer	musim panas	夏天
Sun, the	mata-hari	日頭
Sure	tntu	決斷
Swallow, to	tlan	吞
Swamp	paya	淡水地
Swear, to (take an oath)	bersumpah	咒誓
Swear, to (curse)	kutok	咒讖
Sweep, to	sapu	掃
Sweet	manis	甜
Swell, to	bngkak	腫
Swim, to	bernang	泅
Swing, to	goyang; goyangkan	鞦韆
Sword	pdang	劍
Table	meja	棹
Tail	ekor	尾
Tailor	tukang jait	裁縫

Tailor (Indian)	dhirzi	裁縫
Take, to (fetch)	ambil	携帶
Take, to (carry)	bawa	帶
Take, to (accept)	trima	受
Take away, to	bawa pergi	帶去
Take care, to	jaga	細膩
Take hold of, to	pgang	拎
Take in, to	bawa masok	收入
Take in, to (deceive)	tipu	騙
Take pains, to	buat dngan usaha	做細詳
Take place, to	jadi	成
Take up, to (lift)	angkat	扶起
Tale	cherita	古講
Talk, to	chakap	高
Tall	tinggi	溫
Tame	jinak	絕膽
Tar	minyak tar	油仔味
Taste, to	rasa	糧
Tax	chukai	租地、錢
Tea	ayer teh	茶
Tea leaves	daun teh	葉茶

Teach, to	ajarkan	教先
Teacher	guru	示生
Tear, to	koyak	折講
Tell, to (a tale)	chertrakan	古知
Tell, to (make known)	kasi tau; khabarkan	知地
Temper	prangai	性
Temple (of God)	Ka'abah	殿
Tempt, to	choba	試
Ten	s-puloh	十
Tender (soft)	lmbot	軟
Tender (sore)	sakit	痛
Than	deripada	比
Thank, to	{ balaskan trima kaseh { mnguchap shukor	感恩
Thank you	trima kaseh	感謝
That	itu	彼个
That is to say	ia'itu	就是
Thatch	atap	蓋草
The	itu	彼个
Their; theirs	dia-orang punya	他的
Then (at that time)	waktu itu	當時
Then (after that)	kmdian	然後

There	sana; di-sana; di-situ	彼在
There, to (a place)	k-sana; k-situ	往所
There and back	pergi balik (co')	彼回 諸他
Therefore	sbab itu	以 厚
These	ini	個 賊
They	dia; dia-orang	薄
Thick	tbal	瘦
Thief	pnchuri	事
Thin	nipis; tipis	物
Thin (lean)	kurus	想
Thing (affair)	perkara	務 嘴
Thing (article)	barang	這
Think, to	fikir	刺
Thirsty	haus; dahaga	乾 雖
This	ini	个 一
Thorn	duri	線
Though	mski	三
Thousand, a	s-ribu	罔 座
Thread	bnang	千
Three	tiga	
Throne	takhta	位

Through	trus	過、透
Throw, to	lempar	
Throw away, to	buang	擲
Thumb	ibu jari	頭指
Thunder	guntur; guroh	拇雷
Thus	bgini; dmkian	此如
Tie, to	ikat	、縛
Tiger	herimau	結虎
Tight	trek; knchang	、是
Tile	gnting	縛瓦
Till	sampai	到
Time (in general)	waktu	時
Time (period)	zaman	時
Time (leisure)	smpat	辰閒
Time, olden	zaman dhulu	古
Time (repetition)	kali	昔次
Time, what	pukol brapa	幾
Tin	timah	點錫
Tin (sheet)	timah puteh	白
Tired	pnat	鐵倦
To (a place)	k-	到

To (a person)	k-pada; pada	共
To-day	ini hari	今日
Toe	jari kaki	足指
Together	sama-sama	相與
To-morrow	esok; besok *(co!)*	明日
Tongue	lidah	舌
Too	terlalu; terlampau	太
Too (also)	juga	亦
Tooth	gigi	嘴齒
Toothache	sakit gigi	嘴齒痛
Top	atas; kpala	頂頭、面
Torch	damar; suloh	火把
Total	jmlah	計共
Touch, to	jamah; kna	模
Towards	k-s-blah; ara	對向、面
Towel	tuala	面巾
Town	negri	城
Trade	perniaga'an	生理
Trade, to	berniaga	做生理
Tram	kreta api	火車
Translate, to	salinkan k-bhasa lain	繙譯

Travel, to	berjalan	行路
Tray	dulang	盤
Tread, to	pijak	踏
Tree	poko'; poko' kayu	樹
Trial	bichara	審
Trouble	susah; ksusahan	煩惱
Trowsers	sluar	褌
True	bnar; btul	眞
Truly	s-bnar-nya	實在
Trust, to	harap; perchaya	信靠
Truth	kbnaran; yang bnar	誠實
Try, to	choba	試觀
Try, to (judge)	bicharakan	審案
Tub	tong	桶
Tumble, to	jatoh	跌倒
Tune	lagu	調
Turn, to (return)	balik	返來
Turn, to (upside down)	balikkan	到
Turn, to (revolve)	pusing	轉
Turn, to (cause to revolve)	pusingkan	遨
Turn round, to (change front)	paling; palingkan	越

Turn, to (become)	mnjadi	變
Twelve	dua-blas	十二
Twenty	dua-puloh	二十
Twice	dua-kali	二次
Twig	ranting	樹枝
Twist, to	pintal	鑽
Two	dua	二
Ugly	odoh	歹
Umbrella	payong	雨傘
Unable	ta'boleh	不能
Uncertain	tidak tntu; ta' tntu	無定
Uncle	bapa saudara	伯
Uncomfortable	susah	無快活
Uncommon	jarang	無平常
Uncover, to	buka	掀開
Under	bawah; di-bawah	下底
Under (less than)	kurang deripada	較欠
Underneath	di-bawah	下面
Understand, to	mngerti; tau	曉得
Undo, to	buka; urai	解
Undress, to	buka pakian	脫衫

Unequal	tidak sama	無心相無 平無
Unfair	tidak patut; tidak 'adil	道公
Unhappy	susah-hati; brat-hati	異
Unite, to	hubong; asakan	連
Unjust	tidak bnar	無公無若加至
Unless	kalau tidak	道
Unnecessary	ta'guna	
Until	sampai	
Unto	k-pada; pada	
Untrue	bohong	無
Unusual	jarang	影無 平無
Unwell	sakit	常 病
Unwilling	ta'mau	願甘不無頂
Unwise	bodoh	識智面無頂去
Up	atas; di-atas; k-atas	面頂去設趁
Up, to go	naik	來立頂
Up, to get	bangun	
Up, to set	berdirikan	
Up, to stand	berdiri	立 竪上
Upon	di-atas	
Upper	yang di-atas	頂

Upright (vertical)	berdiri btul	直 倒 反 吊 頂 頂 面 咱 用 熟 路 用 工 貝 錢 重 號	忠 推 倒 慺 去 向 阮 路 用 相 有 無 平 全 無 寶 價 對 值 柔 素 然 若 幾
Upset, to	balikkan		
Upside down	terbalik		
Upside down, to turn	balikkan		
Upstairs	atas		
Upstairs, to go	naik		
Upwards	k-atas		
Us	kita; kami		
Use	guna		
Use, to	pakai; gunakan		
Used to (accustomed)	biasa		
Useful	berguna		
Useless	ta'guna		
Usually	biasa		
Utterly	s-kali-kali; habis		
Vain, in	perchuma		
Valuable	indah; berherga		
Value	herga		
Value, to (highly)	indahkan		
Value, to (fix the price)	nilaikan		
Various	macham-macham		

Varnish	barnis *(col)*	漆
Vary, to	ubah	改
Vegetables	sayur	菜
Very	banyak; terlalu; skali	此不、盡
Victorious, to be	mnang	贏
Village	kampong	社 鄉
Vinegar	chuka	醋
Virgin	anak muda	女 室 在
Visit, to	mlawat	探
Visit, to (call in at)	singgah	
Voice	suara	聲
Vowel points	baris	點字 音 主
Wages	gaji	錢 工
Wail, to	mratap	哭 帝
Wailing	ratap	京 悲
Waist	pinggang	腰
Wait, to	nanti; tunggu	侯 聽
Wait at table, to	jaga meja *(col)*	食 跟 的
Wake, to	bangun; jaga	醒
Wake, to cause to	bangunkan	醒 叫
Walk, to	berjalan	行

Walking-stick	tongkat	拐仔
Wall	tembok; dinding	墙壁、四處
Wander, to	ssat	
Want, to	mau; berkahandak	愛要
Wanting	kurang	欠缺
War	prang	相刣
Warm	panas	燒熱
Warn, to	larangkan; tgahkan	指點
Was	sudah; sudah ada	有會
Wash, to	basoh; mandi; chu chi *(col)*	洗浴
Waste, to	habiskan; buangkan	損
Watch	jam	鏢
Watch, to	jaga; tunggu	看顧
Watchman	orang jaga	更夫仔
Water	ayer	水
Water (for drinking)	ayer minum	飲水
Water carrier	tukang-ayer	挑水者
Wave	ombak	湧
Wax	lilin	蠟
Way	jalan	路行
We	kita; kami	咱阮

Weak	lmah	弱
Wear, to	pakai	穿
Weary	pnat	倦
Wedding	kahwin	婚姻
Week	minggo	一禮拜
Weep, to	mnangis	流目淬
Weigh, to	timbang	稱
Weight	brat	重
Well (of water)	prigi	井
Well (of health)	baik; sehat baik	好
West	barat	西
Wet	basah	濕
Wharf	jmbatan	路頭
What	apa	甚麼
What for	apa sbab	甚麼故
Whatever	barang-apa	不論甚麼
Wheat	gandom	麥
Wheel	roda	輪
When	bila; apabila	何時
When (while)	waktu	時
Where	mana; di-mana; k-mana	在何處

Where from	deri-mana	由何處
Wherever	mana-mana	不拘何所
Whether	kalau; jika	設使
Which	yang	所
Which?	mana? yang mana?	何個一
While, whilst	waktu	何時
Whip	chabok	鞭
Whisper, to	bisek	耳語
White	puteh	白
Whitewash, to	sapu kapur	抹灰
Who	yang	是誰
Who?	siapa	甚誰
Whoever	barang-siapa	不拘誰
Whole (of time)	s-panjang	通全
Whose	siapa punya	是誰的
Why	knapa; apa fasal; apa sbab	何事
Wick	sumbu	紗心
Wicked	jahat	歹
Wickedness	kjahatan	歹
Wide (of space)	luas	濶
Wide (of breadth)	lebar	濶

SINGAPORE TRIGLOT VOCABULARY. 103

Widow	prempuan janda	寡婦
Width	lebar	濶
Wife	bini	妻
Wild	liar	野
Will (future)	nanti; akan	要
Will (to be willing)	mau; suka	肯
Will, the (wish, desire)	kahandak	旨意
Win, to	mnang	贏
Wind	angin	風
Window	jndela	牕仔
Wine	anggor	酒
Wipe, to	sapukan	拭
Wire	dawai	銅線
Wisdom	budi	智識
Wise	berbudi	賢
Wish	kahandak	愛
Wish, to	mau; suka; berkahandak	愛
With	sama; dngan	與
Without (not having)	dngan tiada	無有
Withstand, to	tahan	抵當
Witness	saksi	干證

Woman	prempuan	婦人
Wonder, to	hairan	奇怪
Wood	kayu	柴
Word	perkata'an	話
Work	kerja; pkerja'an	工
Work, to	bkerja	做
Workman	tukang	司
World, the	dunia; bumi	世
Worm (maggot)	ulat	蟲
Worn out	burok	老
Worse	kurang baik; lbeh jahat	更
Worship	smbahyang	拜敬
Worship, to	smbah k-pada	拜敬
Worthy	layak	堪
Wound	luka	傷
Wounded, to be	kna luka	着傷
Wrap up, to	bungkuskan	包
Wrath	marah; murka	怨氣
Wrecked, to be (of ships)	karam	扛破
Write, to	tulis	寫
Write, to (compose)	karang	著冊

Written	tertulis ;tersurat; terkarang	
Wrong	salah	
Yard	ela	
Year	tahun	
Year, new	tahun bharu	
Yeast	ragi	
Yellow	kuning	
Yes	ya	
Yesterday	klmarin ; s-malam	
Yesterday, the day before	klmarin dhulu	
Yield, to	srahkan diri	
Yoke	ko'	
You	angkau; kamu	
Young	muda	
Your	angkau punya	
Youth	orang muda	
Zealous	rajin	

寫不一年明酵黃有昨昨讓駕爾幼汝少熱
了着嗎年　　　　　着、是、　　　車、幼、的年心
　　　　　　　　　　　　　日日　　　　恁細

سسواة يڠد سبوتكن ددالم قرآن درىحال كتاب انجيل دان توريت

A SHORT TREATISE

IN THE MALAY LANGUAGE

on the teaching of the Kora'an with reference to the Bible, with numerous quotations from the Kora'an.

TRANSLATED BY

W. G. SHELLABEAR.

Paper covers 2 cents.

THE SINGAPORE TRIGLOT VOCABULARY.

CONTAINING NEARLY 2,000 WORDS

IN THE

ENGLISH, MALAY AND CHINESE LANGUAGES,

COMPILED BY

W. G. SHELLABEAR.

THE CHINESE RENDERINGS BY

REV. B. F. WEST, M.D.

Paper covers 25 cents, strongly bound in boards 40 cents.

www.ingramcontent.com/pod-product-compliance
Lightning Source LLC
Chambersburg PA
CBHW020148170426
43199CB00010B/947